Survival Self-Defense

**Essential Tips, Facts and Techniques
to Save Your Life**

and

Tactical Kubotan

**23 Strikes for
Powerful Self-Defense**

KIT CRUMB

Lost Lodge Press, Ashland Oregon

DISCLAIMER - PLEASE READ:

The self-defense techniques in this book can cause serious physical injury. **They are intended to be used only for self-defense in order to protect the practitioner from harm by an assailant.** Kit Crumb and Black Dragon Self-defense assume no responsibility for injury or damage resulting from the execution of the techniques and exercises presented in this book.

Table of Contents

Introduction

DID YOU KNOW THAT HAVING and projecting confidence will cause a criminal to back down more quickly than any "attitude" or fighting technique? And that projecting an attitude that says "stay away from me" can actually invite an attack?

True confidence is backed by training, but it isn't the length of the training that counts, it's the formidable effectiveness of tactics and techniques that can be deeply and easily learned—ready for immediate and powerful response—that will make the difference.

Knowing how to NOT become a victim includes training in self-defense techniques and some understanding of the criminal mind and his strategies to overwhelm, hurt or rob you. Having the confidence that you're well prepared is priceless.

Welcome to *Survival Self-Defense.* This book is about body weapons, attack methods, and vulnerable targets. In a sense surviving an attack begins and ends with the mind. Avoiding attack altogether involves "Situational Awareness"; that is, awareness and evaluation of your immediate situation. This comes through training the five senses (or six) through cultivation of mindfulness, the mind. Control of fear certainly comes into play before and during an attack. Science states that we can never eliminate fear but through mental training and acquired self confidence you can control it. The motivation and perseverance to learn physical moves that will stop an attack until those moves

> In a sense surviving an attack begins and ends with the mind. Avoiding attack altogether involves "Situational Awareness"; that is, awareness and evaluation of your immediate situation.

are cellular, begins in the mind. You can see that awareness, being fearless, and ingrained knowledge of fighting techniques all start with the mind.

Through mastery of these three skills—awareness, the ability to channel fear, and solid knowledge of self-defense techniques—you have the basics of *Survival Self-Defense.*

Through "Situational Awareness" you will learn how to avoid an attack. By controlling fear you will be able to focus on stopping the aggression and allowing your knowledge of physical moves to play out in a way that will disable your opponent. Combined, these three skills will, in the event of an unavoidable attack, stop the aggression, subdue your opponent, keep you out of harm's way while providing a chance to escape. *Survival Self-Defense* isn't about violence. It is about the cultivation of personal empowerment. Through heightened awareness, the control of fear, and mastery of the physical you will gain self confidence.

Channeling Fear

WHAT CAUSES FEAR? It could be high places, dogs or even public speaking that bring on that stomach churning, nerve tingling, paralyzing sensation. Fear is a normal emotional response to external sources of danger. It is considered the strongest of the emotions, but it is just that, an emotion. The most common symptoms of fear are rapid breathing and increased heart rate. This occurs when the body dumps excessive amounts of adrenaline into the blood, preparing the body for fight or flight. But like the emotions of anger or jealousy we can choose not to be afraid.

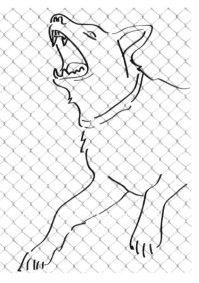

For instance, you walk past a yard, and a big German Shepherd suddenly charges the fence, barking furiously. You choose not to be afraid because you know the fence will keep him in his yard. Still, your pulse races as you increase your pace when he charges, but you're really not afraid.

No matter how secure you feel knowing he is behind a sturdy hurricane metal fence, your body still picks up on the potential danger and dumps extra adrenaline into your bloodstream. You will always experience a little rapid breathing no matter how much you assure yourself that the dog can't hurt you. But before you know it, you're walking past the yard without batting an eye. Why? You have channeled your fear. He may catch you off guard on occasion, and boost your pulse, but the effect of the "startle response" is short lived and controlled.

Now, lets take the art of channeling fear to the next level.

A 48 year old business woman has agreed to meet a friend at a new restaurant, but she's unfamiliar with that part of town. When she walks out of the parking garage, one look at the buildings and the derelict cars and she realizes she should have asked a few more questions before agreeing to meet. With a brisk step she turns down the sidewalk in the direction of the restaurant and within a couple of blocks has begun to relax as the image of fine wine and the great cuisine she'll enjoy in the company of her friend fills her mind.

The sound of a shuffling step brings her out of her reverie. A quick glance at her reflection in a store window and her heart skips a beat. Not ten feet behind her is a rough looking man in a leather jacket. She regulates her breathing as she leaves the reflection behind, now only able to track him by the sound of his step and labored breathing as he approaches. Aware of the effects of the adrenaline rush – faster than usual reflex and more power to her punch– she mentally readies herself with images of delivering devastating strikes for a quick escape. Suddenly he's next to her, shuffling along, hurrying to get somewhere, staring at his shoes.

He never gives her a second glance. She stifles a sigh of relief and slows her pace to put some distance between her and the man in the leather jacket. She watches as he turns down an alley. When she looks up the street, she sees her friend standing in the middle of the sidewalk, shading her eyes from the sun and looking in her direction. "Hello, I'm so glad you made it," her friend says. "A lot of my friends won't venture into this part of town, but believe me the food here makes it worth it." Our business woman smiles and turns to look into the restaurant only to see her own reflection, relaxed and at ease. "Oh it was only a couple blocks."

When she first noticed the leather clad stranger our business woman experienced the startle effect of a rapid pulse. However, understanding the positive effects of the adrenaline rush she experienced, she took control of her breathing and created positive images of her escape. She channeled her fear. Instead of overreacting to a racing pulse with visions of beatings and rape, she took control, knowing that if it did come down to a confrontation she'd have the advantage.

Somewhere in her background she trained in a practical self-defense system that stressed the value of coming from a calm center, and that led her to believe she was equipped to cope with an unknown attack.

Now it's your turn.

Before you can channel fear you first have to know what you're afraid of. That's easy. The focus of this section is on channeling the fear of being attacked, generally the fear of being physically injured for the purpose of robbery. Fear of injury can be anything from being pushed to the ground and scraping your hands and knees to being pounded into submission with a club or raped or anything in between.

In the first example the fear of dogs was channeled because of the big metal fence. In the case of our business woman she was able to channel her fear because she understood the physical sensations brought on by adrenaline and she had trained in self-defense. In both examples the heart raced and breathing became rapid but the individuals recognized these as symptoms of an adrenaline rush. Another example would be when driving, and another driver runs a red light missing your car by inches, or anytime you are thrust into an unexpected situation you perceive as dangerous. Fortunately, the nature of an attack is based on a fairly simple premise: whatever the attacker is going to do, he has to touch you first. Remember that you are not going to engage the attacker in combat, you're going to stop his aggression or redirect it.

It is imperative that you believe that your self-defense arsenal *will* enable you to deal with an attack to a predictable end, and that the attacker won't be able to get past your self-defense moves. You will be fighting for your life.

But before you psyche-up for a confrontation, you want to give yourself every chance to avoid an attack altogether.

Seeing

THERE ARE NO PHANTOM MUGGERS. By this I mean that no one suddenly appears out of thin air grabbing punching or pushing you. Yes, there's always the chance of being blindsided, attacked from behind. However, statistically the attacker reveals his intentions, often for the sake of intimidation. Even if he came out from behind something or stepped out of an alley moving rapidly in your direction there is still that moment, or two before first contact. "Seeing" is literally evaluating the attacker for available targets – and it takes only a second. Between the time when he steps into the open and the first moment of contact, you mentally take a snapshot of the attacker.

Seeing is literally evaluating the attacker for available targets —and it takes only a second.

If you're trained in a practical self-defense system, you understand the concept of body weapons. You know how to strike with speed and power. First, however you must locate your targets – you must "see". The following example demonstrates how seeing affects the outcome of an attack.

You're walking through a park alone and first hear the attacker approach. You turn to face the sound of footsteps and rough talk, initially out of curiosity. Before you can size up the situation, literally in a single heart beat, your body is flooded with adrenaline, the "startle effect." Then you see. He's leading with his chin, scowling and mouthing profanities. His eyes and ears are the available targets. In the blink of an eye he's wadded up your blouse in both fists and is shaking you like a rag doll. Cupping your hands, you slap his ears, rupture his ear drums, and make your escape.

Sounds good, but let's back up and change the attackers appearance.

Your jogging through the park this time, and the attacker steps out from behind a tree. His hair is shoulder length, as he approaches, he whips it back and forth intended to intimidate. At a glance your available targets are the eyes and throat. In a moment he has a massive hand wrapped around your shoulder and is pulling back a balled up fist. With adrenaline propelled speed you thrust your right palm against the left side of his face, thumb against his eye, and follow his head, as he twists it back and forth trying to escape the pressure of your thumb.

Seeing occurs because you know your targets and in the blink of an eye you're able to determine which ones are available for attack. From the moment you notice the attacker, to first contact, to your escape may only be a matter of seconds if you learn how to locate targets by seeing them.

Wouldn't it be nice if you could avoid an attack altogether? There is a way, and that's what we'll look at next.

Situational Awareness

SITUATIONAL AWARENESS is being aware of what is happening around you, and understanding how this information will impact your goals and objectives, both now and in the immediate future, which in turn dictates your actions.

"Situational Awareness" is used by the military and your local police department. It works for anyone encountering a rapid change of events that could impact one's goal. In other words, it can work for everyone. Your goal may be as simple as walking from the parking lot to work, a route that takes you past a half dozen panhandlers. It could be as complex as taking a vacation by yourself, or driving cross-country to a new job. (Watch the movie Breakdown for that storyline).

What can you do to reduce the odds of becoming a victim? Becoming aware of the way you carry yourself, being alert and not distracted (by a cell phone, for example), and walking with purpose. All of these suggestions are helpful when crossing into what I call the "zone of danger," walking past half a dozen homeless men, crossing a parking lot to your car in the dark, jogging through the park by yourself. The list goes on and on.

You may not have to cross into that zone though, and that's where this multi-layered awareness plays a vital role. But "Situational Awareness" isn't something you switch on only when you're about to cross into that "zone of danger," when you notice the panhandlers leaning on your car. It's a preventive something you do before you leave the house for your morning walk, before you lock your car to cross the parking lot, before you leave work at the end of the day. These are the casual moments when "Situational Awareness" can pay off.

There's one other consideration before you enter that "zone of danger," and that's your "Code of Conduct". I'm not talking about your moral compass; I'm referring to the changes you're willing to make in your daily routine. When you notice the homeless men around your car, do you just shrug and head out anyway, or do you go back into the building and get a fellow employee to walk you to your car. What is your personal code? What has to happen before you'll change your route, or change your mind?

Let's combine these two strong preventives, "Situational Awareness" and "Code of Conduct", in a common scenario – flying.

A pilot scans the horizon and immediate air space constantly. He may see some small clouds and press on, they're not likely to cause any problems. "Situational Awareness" is his seeing the clouds and deciding whether they will cause him to alter his route to reach his goal, that is, his destination. His "Code of Conduct" is his willingness to alter his route just in case the clouds contain foul weather. He continues on, and indeed the little clouds are just innocent puffs of moisture. But on the other side of the little guys he discovers big black thunderheads. His "Situational Awareness" tells him that whatever resides within those skyscraper-size clouds could cause real navigational problems. His "Code of Conduct" tells him that the time saved by continuing through the clouds might not be worth the risk, and he changes course.

How "Situational Awareness" and "Code of Conduct" work in a different scenario.

You park in the same city lot each day and cross it to the little bridge that goes over the creek and leads to the path that takes you to the building where you work. Each day it's the same old thing. As you approach the bridge there's a homeless man who tracks your progress with his eyes hoping for a handout. You ignore him, and press on. No problem. You look forward to the little walk and although the homeless man is a concern, he's not a problem.

But today is different.

As you leave the relative safety of the parking lot and the bridge comes into view, there's a cluster of homeless men gathered at the far end of the bridge. "Situational Awareness" kicks in and you realize that the time you save getting to work by going over the bridge might not be worth the risk. But it's your "Code of Conduct" that keeps you from rationalizing that this is just a friendly gathering, and guides you to the decision to backtrack to the parking lot where you'll take the long way to work, arriving a couple of minutes late, but unscathed. "Situational Awareness" alerted you to a potential danger, but it was your personal "Code of Conduct" that turned you around.

As you sit at work, you remember with a shiver that for a second you considered crossing the bridge. Although you're pretty sure nothing would have happened, you're pleased with yourself that you didn't take the risk.

There are four levels of "Situational Awareness", lets take a look at how you might apply these levels in your daily life.

You're going to meet your wife, who's out shopping at her favorite shop. As you lock your car and head out onto the sidewalk you're in **Level One**; your aware of your immediate surroundings both in the parking lot and along the sidewalk. You've got about six blocks to walk and are enjoying the exercise when you notice some dark thunderheads gathering, you wonder if you'll make the remaining four blocks before it begins to rain. You are now in **Level Two**; aware of the presence of a vague threat that hasn't appeared yet, but you're certainly on alert. Two blocks to go and you notice a few drops on the sidewalk and a couple that hit you on the head, so you pick up your pace and begin to look for shelter. You're determined to make the shop. You're now in **Level Three;** alert for the downpour, scanning shops for an awning, lengthening your stride. Suddenly lightening cracks and the skies open up. In a heart beat you move to **Level Four** and sprint to a nearby awning, avoiding the threat of being soaked to the skin.

Our example seems simple enough. But how often have you heard someone say that they were surprised by the weather and caught in the rain, or caught in a speed trap, or even shocked when they balanced their checkbook? Honestly? Most situations we encounter throughout our day have signposts leading up to them; you just have to know how to read the signs.

The same is true with attacks on your person. As I said before, there are no phantom muggers. These people that mean you harm don't just materialize in front of you. They may step out of the shadows, or out from behind cars or buildings. It may even be the guy coming your way on the sidewalk who seems consumed with his newspaper. If it's dusk and the shadows are getting longer and darker, go to **Level Two,** change your route to one more heavily traveled, or where street lights eliminate the shadows. If the sidewalk follows a line of buildings, and they usually do, switch to **Level Two**. Move to the outside of the sidewalk and assume a threat is present, but you haven't seen it yet. If you find that your route will put you past a van or old school bus, bump up to **Level Three**, anticipate danger, and cross the street or give the vehicle a wide berth.

The "Survivor Mindset"

"Situational Awareness" doesn't mean you'll never be attacked, and it doesn't mean walking around in a perpetual state of paranoia. It simply means that you've changed the odds of being surprised by the unexpected by staying aware of your immediate environment. It's now time to change your mind. We often read in the newspaper about the victim of a violent crime but the story seldom tells of the pain and suffering of their relatives, or how victims often experience financial problems from time lost from work to handle legal, insurance, and other problems associated with being a victim. Remember, the attacker has no compunction about taking your cash and credit cards, beating you into submission, or raping you. It's often said that if you survive an attack and the mugger is caught, he goes to jail and you go to a counselor.

However, having the "Survivor Mindset" can change that. The attacker may still go to jail but you will get on with your life. When I get to the part about the five vulnerable targets and how to attack them you may cringe. *But when you consider the physical mental and emotional damage you may suffer from an attack* you'll want to read the section over several times.

The "Survivor Mindset" simply means that you will do whatever it takes to survive. You will not be controlled by fear, you will lash out with a righteous indignation, unleashing devastating and possibly lethal responses to intended aggression.

The "Survivor Mindset" simply means that you will do whatever it takes to survive. You will not be controlled by fear, you will lash out with a righteous indignation, unleashing devastating and possibly lethal responses to intended aggression. When presented with the body's physiological response to danger of fight or flight, you will always choose to flee. *But should there be no exit route and you* *have to fight, you will use sophisticated training and your "Survivor Mindset" to defeat an attacker's brutish methods.*

The "Survivor Mindset" begins with the statement that you will not be controlled by fear.

We've talked about channeling fear, but what exactly are we afraid of? Most often it is fear of the unknown that brings on the inability to react. What does he want? What will he do to me? Will he leave me alone if I comply? If I tell him to leave me alone will he go? If I scream like a Banshee will he go? The fear of a negative answer to any of these can bring on hyperventilation, and constriction of veins and capillaries that can actually result in narrowed vision, an inability to talk (or scream), and even fainting due to reduced circulation. These are all responses the mugger wants to trigger. To eliminate the façade of fear that protects the mugger/attacker, Let's clear away the fear of the unknown by examining the seven most important traits of the mugger.

1. **Muggers aren't always grubby** looking or shabbily dressed.

2. **Muggers range from educated,** having gone to college, to suffering from mental deficiencies.

3. **Muggers have no compassion or empathy** for their victims. Their skill sets are often well honed. They may include picking a victim, choosing a location for the assault, and even deciding ahead of time how best to render the victim helpless.

5. **Muggers may dress to enhance their physique** in an attempt to intimidate a victim, or dress in layers to appear larger and more ferocious then they actually are.

6. **Muggers may not speak or may blister the air with abusive language** intended to threaten the victim.

7. **Muggers are often motivated by delusions of grandeur** that elevate rape to gratifying sex, and the acquisition of money to the resolution of problems and the elevation of prestige.

What can we take away from these seven traits? The mugger may vary in size, dress, language, and intelligence, but has a strong motivation and a tendency toward violence and intimidation, even when it's not necessary. He lacks compassion for his victim and operates from a mental and emotional reality that is completely different from yours.

By having a real image of the mugger we strip away a fear of the unknown.

Unfortunately, women's self-defense courses rarely address more then the actual attack. Wouldn't it be better to avoid the attack altogether? Let's cover the four most important points of conduct that will make you someone a mugger would be less likely to choose as his next victim.

- **Walk with purpose, with a brisk pace,**
  Walk as if you have a destination where people are waiting for you. According to FBI files the mugger is looking for someone ambling along, seemingly with no particular place to go.

- **Walk tall with good posture.**
  Muggers watch for a specific type to avoid – a confident posture indicates a physicality that might not be easy to subdue.

- **Eliminate potential "handles," such as hands in pockets or holding a cell phone.**
  Secure your purse under the arm, muggers look for a purse strap to grab and keep your hands free, arms swinging naturally.

- **Be alert. This means no cell phone, texting or bluetooth conversations, and, yes, jogging or walking while listening to an ipod makes you more vulnerable.**
  Muggers watch for someone who is preoccupied or self absorbed. Surprise is his greatest advantage.

Practice these four points – they'll help keep you safe

We've now seen the mugger/attacker for what he is, a brutal dispassionate opportunist motivated by delusions of grandeur. Is he unpredictably dangerous? Yes. But is he unstoppable? Absolutely not.

Body Weapons and the Four Vulnerable Targets

Body weapons are the weapons you carry around with you all the time; fist, palm, fingers, edge of the hand, and elbow. Notice that I didn't include the knee, there are several reasons for this. The knee is a good weapon but it is poorly placed, and to use the knee you would have to have an available target.

The only target that is at a good striking level for the knee is the groin, and the groin is a poor target. I can hear the gasps of disbelief, so let me explain why.

The location of the testicles is behind the penis and slightly back from front. They are soft and contained in a sac that can easily move forward and back or side to side. The testicles are further protected by jeans and possibly underwear. This makes the testicles a tough target. The way to hit the groin (testicles) would be an upward strike originating from between the legs. This would force them up into the pelvic floor, the pain would be excruciating, indeed debilitating. If you managed to knee an opponent in the groin, the rounded knee would force the testicles back at best.

> The only target that is at a good striking level for the knee is the groin, and the groin is a poor target. I can hear the gasps of disbelief, so let me explain why.

For the knee to become a viable weapon your attacker would have to be pressed up against you so that the strike would come up from directly underneath, forcing the testicles up. If, however, your attacker had his body pressed against you it would be late in the attack. And since a knee attack to the groin is risky at best it would be better to go for a target that is more of a sure thing. The groin is not a good target because it is easily and instinctively protected, it is therefore a moving target. The knee is not a good weapon because there is only one viable target: the groin. And to use the knee leaves you standing on one foot.

The fist, palm, fingers, edge of the hand, and elbow are all good weapons because you have two sets of each. The hand has extreme extension forward, up and down, left and right. This large range of motion make a variety of targets within easy reach. The hand can strike quickly and be retracted just as fast. The elbow is your fifth weapon of choice. It has less range of motion than the hand, but because of its hard boney nature can be deadly.

Now that we know our best body weapons and why, let's move on to targets.

Consider that during a confrontation targets may appear and then move out of range in a matter of seconds. **So viable targets are those that are within reach for more than a split second or that move slowly.** When struck, a target must debilitate the attacker. It must be difficult for him to protect. Based on these criteria there are four targets to consider: **eyes, ears, throat, and pubic bone.** The four targets used in *Survival Self-Defense* are always present and almost always within reach. They take little force to create disabling effects, and they don't rely on pain to disable.

You know what your body weapons are, lets take a close look at the four targets.

CAUTION:

Before you read the devastating medical implications of striking the four targets, remember that these are worst case scenarios.

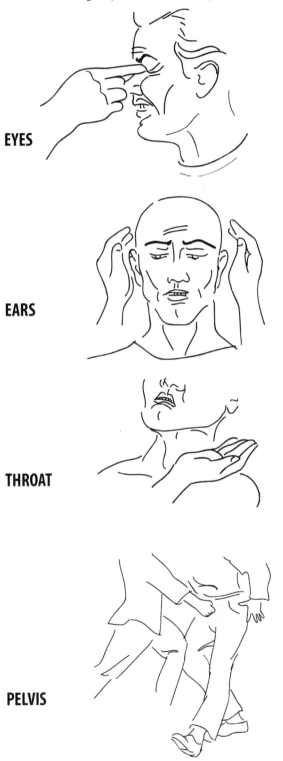

EYES

EARS

THROAT

PELVIS

THE EYES

The eye can be struck most easily with the index finger or the thumb.

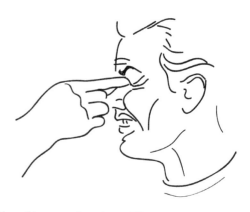

Medical implications:

Rupture of the eye bulb with protrusion of the watery and gelatinous like contents will result when the bulb is no longer able to withstand the direct piercing. Temporary or permanent blindness is the common result. Tremendous shocking pain will occur. An uncontrollable watering of the eyes will always take place.

The scenario

You're walking across the parking lot in broad daylight, the attacker steps out from behind a van. His hair is shoulder length, his clothes are loose but not shabby. His eyes are drilling holes in you, he means to intimidate. At a glance your available targets are the eyes and throat, but he's taller than you thought, and as he nears and looks down at you his throat becomes protected by his chin. In a moment he has grabbed your shoulder and cocked back his hand for a slap. With adrenaline propelled speed you thrust your right palm against the left side of his face, thumb against his eye. He turns his head sharply to break loose, but he's close enough that you're able to follow the movement. He attempts the slap, but you increase the pressure on his eye until his only escape is to back out of your reach. **When he steps away you make your escape.**

COMMENTARY

In most cases an index finger to the eye would be difficult if the attacker were holding still. However, in close contact it might work, although the thumb is less likely to rupture the eye.

The scenario from the attacker's point of view

The attacker is 6'3" and has been involved in athletics. He's used to getting his way through intimidation and if that doesn't work, brute force. He's been targeting people in parking lots across town. Most of his intended victims were easily intimidated when he strolled up to within inches of them, stared down and made his demands for cash or credit cards. He plans on leaving town tomorrow. This is his last victim from the area so he's feeling okay with violence if it goes that far. When he steps out from behind the van he decides to really mess up this victim. In six strides he's within inches, grabs the shoulder and pulls his hand back for a real slap. He's surprised when his victim reacts with a thumb to his eye, the slap will stop that. When the pressure increases he snaps his head to one side and on second thought balls his slapping hand into a fist, but the pressure increases. He steps back and clasps his hand to his eye in pain.

COMMENTARY:

How an attacker reacts to pain will be determined by the degree of his sobriety. If the attacker hadn't backed off with medium pressure to his eye, it would be an indicator that he was under the influence of drugs or alcohol. It might have been necessary to step into the attacker and straighten the arm driving the pressure and the pain to a debilitating extreme.

By placing the fingers on the side of the attackers head placement of the thumb on the eye is easier to maintain.

THE EARS

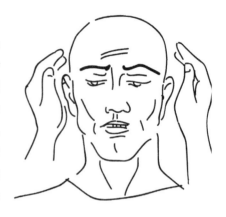

Palm striking on both sides of the head simultaneously will act to stabilize the head and therefore will double the percussive impact on the ears. The tympanic membrane (ear drum) will rupture from the volume of air forced through the external auditory canal. Capillaries inside the canal will be ruptured and swell. Loss of hearing could be temporary depending on total injury based on the volume of air forced into the auditory canal. There will be extreme and debilitating pain with shock as a possible immediate result.

The scenario

Your employer is having the company parking lot repaved and for the past month you, and the rest of the staff, have been using the public parking garage three blocks away. It's taken some getting used to but you've become comfortable parking in the cavernous underground lot, and actually enjoy walking the three blocks to work with fellow employees. But today is different. In order to finish your project on schedule you've had to come in on Saturday, alone. The garage is nearly empty, but a number of vehicles have already taken the spots near the exit. You park as close as you can. Before you get out of your car you look all around, the garage seems empty. As soon as you get out, you lock your car, instantly wishing the keyless locking device didn't beep.

You walk past the line of vehicles headed for the exit, mind on finishing your project, but your distraction is broken by the echo of foot falls that aren't yours. A large white delivery van is the only vehicle between you and the exit. You quicken your pace. Suddenly you're pushed from behind so hard that you slam into the side of the van. Before you can react a powerful grip on your shoulder spins you around. You're looking directly into the smirking face of your attacker. Both his hands lash out, palms open, shoving you against the van. In a heartbeat **you cup both hands and, adrenaline pumping, clap them hard over his ears.** In a roar of pain he pushes you to the ground then staggers back, hands held to either side of his head. **You now have a chance to make an escape.**

COMMENTARY
Although a single slap to one ear might have caused the attacker to back off, striking both ears simultaneously guaranteed a debilitating result.

The scenario from the attacker's point of view.
The attacker isn't tall or big and knows it. He uses violence to control his intended victims, and seeks out dark or out of the way locations for his attacks. But his trip through the parking garage was for the purpose of breaking into cars, he was interrupted when you drove in. He quickly stepped behind one of the giant cement support pillars, knowing you'd head straight for the exit.

Everything was perfect, the parking garage was empty and his intended victim was alone. In three quick strides he'd be able to shove her face first into the van, spin her around and slam her again, she'd never have a chance. He'd grinned at how he'd gotten you by surprise, and when he spun you around, just as planned, looked you right in the eye and, stepping closer to make it more powerful, pushed you again. He was about to push you to the ground when you slapped his ears. He managed a weak shove but was distracted by the piercing pain.

COMMENTARY

The intended victim was able to apply the strike to the ears only because she kept her cool through the attack. Although the eyes were available he might have been to close to make an eye poke work. Because of training she was able to access the targets and make the right decision.

THE THROAT

A strike with the side of the hand to the side or front of the throat could result in some or all of the following:

1. Contusion of the internal Jugular vein
2. Contusion of the vagus nerve
3. Hematoma (blood) in the carotid sheath
4. Fracture of the cartilage protecting the larynx

There are two branches of the vagus nerve, one on each side of the neck. Injury to one may not be fatal. Damage to one side of the nerve could cause spasms of the lungs and heart, creating shortness of breath and heart palpitations.

The Scenario

A fellow martial artist from Anchorage told me the following story about a friend who owned a martial art school there. One evening, his bookkeeper, who was NOT a martial artist, had collected the receipts for the past couple of days and exited the dojo through the rear into the alley where he was parked. It was his habit to take cash and checks home with him on Wednesdays, and make the deposit first thing Thursday morning. This had been his routine for over a year. He had tucked the deposits in an envelope and placed it in his briefcase.

He had walked the dozen or so steps from the exit to his car, and already had his keys in hand when he was attacked. He was struck in the lower back so hard he began to pass out, as the briefcase was ripped from his hand and he felt his legs begin to give out. He turned and executed a "karate chop" (the only martial art move he knew) to the side of the attacker's neck. The bookkeeper fell to the ground unconscious — but so did the attacker.

COMMENTARY

The bookkeeper had been struck with a two-by-four across the lower back, hitting his kidney. The attacker suffered a slight contusion to the jugular vein but suffered a concussion when he fell and his head hit the ground. Unfortunately, I don't have the attacker's perspective on the this but I felt it was worth relating here because the bookkeeper, **a soft spoken, middle-age man who'd never been in a fight in his life and had never studied martial arts or taken a self-defense course yet was able to execute an effective chop to the neck.**

PELVIS & PUBIS

The pelvis is a basin-shaped structure that supports the spinal column and protects the abdominal organs, and is actually two separate bones connected by the sacrum at the back and the pubis in the front. The pubic bone isn't really a bone at all, but a wedge of cartilage. Behind the pubic bone and slightly above is the bladder.

The pain from a forceful strike to the pubic bone may create nerve trauma that can radiate to the inner thighs making it difficult to stand. Secondary to nerve trauma, but no less severe, a strike to the pubis can result in a punctured intestine and possible ruptured bladder, either of which would result in hemorrhage and immediate shock.

The Scenario

You're a health conscious individual and enjoy aerobic classes and long walks. You work on the fifth floor of an eighteen story building. When you get to work and are confronted in the lobby with a sign declaring the elevator out of service for the next seven days due to maintenance, your happy to take the stairs. After several days it becomes a routine. The stairs are concrete with slip-proof edges. The landings at each floor are well illuminated and have railings.

During the morning, at lunch, and at break time the stairs are alive with employes, but today you were sent to the seventh floor on an errand. You exit the hall to the stairs and head back down. When you reach the sixth floor platform you pass a man heading up, you smile and he nods and returns the smile. Only two steps off the platform you're nearly lifted off your feet by your hair. Turning around you glimpse the face of the smiling man you passed only moments ago as you execute a palm thrust into his pubic bone. His expelled air comes out in a groan as he releases your hair and crumples to the step. **You run for an exit.**

COMMENTARY

In this particular case the strike to the pubic bone was easy because the attacker was a step higher then his intended victim. But even had the attack occurred on level ground it only would have required a slight crouch to be in reach of the target.

The scenario from the attacker's point of view

The attacker is nondescript and doesn't draw much attention to himself. He's held various jobs around town and even in some of the buildings of the business district. He moves around the state a lot, not so much looking for work as trying to avoid authorities. He considers himself a carnal beast and knows that if caught he'll be labeled a sexual predator. He can't hold down a job and he's bored. When he applied at the plaza building and noticed the elevator out of service he began to hang out in the stairwells between breaks and lunch to avoid crowds. His methods are intentionally brutal to get fast compliance. He carries a pair of medical scissors to cut away clothes and further intimidate. He's making his last trip up and only plans on going to the tenth floor when he hears someone coming; he checks to make sure the scissors are out of sight. When he sees it's a woman, head down apparently deep in thought, he goes into his act. She looks up as they pass and he nods and smiles to set her at ease, then one more step, whirls, grabs her hair, lifts and pulls. To his utter surprise she turns and thrusts her palm forward. Thinking she's trying to hit him in the groin, he attempts to cut the movement short and gives her hair a yank. Too late. Suddenly his bladder feels full and tendrils of pain shoot into his thighs and up into his lower abdomen.

COMMENTARY

The attacker might have avoided the palm thrust to the pelvic bone but his intended victim was able to gauge the viability of the target. The attacker profile came from the FBI Uniform Crime Reports for profile of a sexual predator .

Now, let's take a look at a more complex attack and response situation.

 You're taken totally by surprise by an attack from behind where the assailant grabs you by the shoulders. Your first response is to step forward with your left foot the instant you feel hands on your shoulders. WHY? This puts you in a stable position and it stretches out the attackers arms. Now, without pause you do two things at once. Without moving your feet, you turn clockwise 180 degrees and simultaneously drive your right arm straight up. As you finish your turn you drive your elbow down as though you want to slam it into your own right hip. Your descending elbow will accomplish one of two things. Certainly it will collide with your attackers arms. Will this make him let go? Probably not. You will more than likely end up with one of his arms trapped between your right side and right arm. More important is the event this movement brings about. When you step and turn it not only straightens the attackers arms but hyper-extends his left arm because it's pulling him, and his head ends up inches from your right hand after you've finished your turn and completed your elbow move. Now you can deliver a single palm thrust to the chin of a slightly off balance attacker. I guarantee it will hit home. Now, turn and run.

Lets look at the same event from the attacker's point of view.

Without being noticed our attacker sneaks up behind his intended victim (it's a low traffic area). He wants to grab her by the shoulders and spin her around. He gets as close as he can without being noticed, somewhere around twelve inches or so. He wants to be close enough so when he turns her around he can easily grab her, take control. He has barely had time to wad her blouse into his grip when she lunges forward. His first impression is that she is trying to run away, but he has a handful of her clothes so she's not going anywhere. He lurches forward a bit in order to maintain his grip, but she's smaller then he is, he's got her for sure. When she spins around he really tightens his grip, expecting her to fight to get loose. Her elbow slams down on his arm, and he's ticked off now. But before he can let go to slap her silly he's slammed with a palm to the chin. His head snaps back he bites his tongue, chips a tooth, and gets a case of whiplash. But what if the attacker had released his grip when she turned around? In that case she would have attacked one of two targets, the eyes or the throat, whichever was more available.

COMMENTARY

Ok, alright, I admit it. I added that last part about being a mouth breather for effect. But as you can see, our intended victim doesn't try to fight him, or surprise him into running away because of her ferocity. Exactly how did she make this work? Why didn't she explode on this guy like a Tasmanian Devil? When the attacker grabbed her from behind, in a move of total surprise she responded from a place of calm self confidence. The move worked because it was simple and the intended victim had practiced it over and over until it was second nature, and she was confident that she could perform every step of the technique. Still you ask, how did she build that confidence and what was the process for learning the move?

The learning process and mastering this material, creates personal self empowerment and confidence and can be completed in three steps.

1. **The first step is going through the motions** and getting a sense of the movement necessary to execute the self-defense tactic.

2. **The second step is working with someone bigger** and stronger than you, who can progressively increase the intensity as you become more efficient, and make the attack situation more realistic.

3. **The important third step is keeping the material fresh in your mind.** Once learned, it only takes a walk-through to trigger muscle memory and bring back the mental components surrounding an attack.

Now that we've taken an in depth look at body weapons and targets, let's look at the "Five Myths" about targets and attacks.

Five Common
Self-defense Myths

Myth #1

Your anger— going ballistic, combined with specific moves, will subdue your opponent.

Fact

Rage has no place in a self-defense situation. In contrast, being prepared with a response based on knowledge, practice and strategic evaluation gives you a better chance of defeating your opponent. A thrashing display of anger not only dilutes any response, but indicates to the attacker a level of desperation.

Myth #2

Stomp on the attacker's instep to hobble him.

Fact

If your attacker is standing perfectly still, stomping on his foot will work...to really tick him off. Attackers like to strike fear into their intended female victims. They'll charge or grab, constantly moving to assert their dominance. Will you really have the presence of mind to locate his foot, and transfer all your weight forward or back? Oops that will put you inches away from a raging bull!

Myth #3

Knee the attacker in the groin to put him out of action.

Fact

Most men have been protecting their groin all of their lives. Some muggers when apprehended were actually found to be wearing an athletic cup – they expected an attack to the groin and were prepared for it.

Myth #4

Palm to the face to drive him back.

Fact

Many attackers have grown up in rough situations where learning the rudiments of boxing was natural. Protecting their head with their arms, or turning their head to ward off a punch, slap, or palm thrust is second nature.

Myth #5

Multiple strikes will keep an attacker off balance.

Fact

Many attackers want a submissive victim so as not to attract attention. When you deliver a flurry of strikes he may double or triple his efforts, striking out with devastating speed and power in hopes of subduing his victim (you) before someone notices.

A last word on responding with multiple strikes:

The mugger/attacker is no fool. He isn't going to let you repeatedly strike at his face or any other target. He knows as well as you that one of those strikes is likely to reach its target and you can bet that he will stop the onslaught any way he can — which usually means a super violent intervention. You may argue that if your attacks are delivered, one on top of the other, so fast that he has no choice but to retreat.

Wrong!

The time that exists between each strike is all the attacker needs to insert himself and break the pattern. If he's slow or on drugs he'll revert to the only thing he knows to break the series of strikes, brute force.

Repetitive strikes do not work!

Resistance and going head-to-head with the attacker does not work.

Tactical Kubotan

23 Strikes for
Powerful Self-Defense

THE GREATEST FEATURE OF THE KUBOTAN is that you can strike hard virtually anywhere on the body and it will hurt like hell!

But knowing where your assailant's most vulnerable areas are increases your odds of disabling him so that you can get away. That's the thing to remember – turn and run! With the kubotan, your weapons are surprise and extreme pain, temporarily disabling the attacker. This gives you a priceless opportunity to turn and run.

Imagine this scenario... you're jogging early in the morning when the streets are quiet. You hear someone running up behind you and suddenly a person grabs you and tries to take you down. You have only your strength and skill to fight back – and if that isn't your strong suit, you're in trouble.

But now, imagine that you're carrying a kubotan (for joggers we recommend slipping a kubotan into your watchband which makes it very easy to grab). You pull out the kubotan and strike - the top of the hands! Back of the thigh! Face! Arms! Your assailant is surprised by painful strikes and is suddenly faced with an opponent who is armed and can inflict injury! You now have an opportunity to run, and since you're already good at this –YOU GET AWAY!

Introduction

The assailant encountered most often by untrained citizens uses simple strong-arm tactics, that is, a push, punch, slap, grab, or body hold, like a bear hug or head lock, to bring a victim to submission, therefore Kubotan is best used against torso, arms, hands, head, face and throat.

The twenty-three strike points endorsed in this booklet will result in excruciating and often debilitating pain, but are not pressure points. These points have been chosen because they are the most easily accessible during a street attack.

Before learning the target zones memorize the following terms for motions:

Arc: refers to the bend of your arm.

Rising arc: refers to the upward motion of your hand while the arm remains bent.

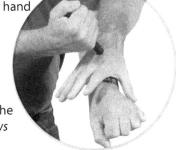

Falling arc: refers to the downward motion of your hand while the arm remains in an arc.

Near chest: is the basic position. The Kubotan is an inch or so out from your chest. Your arm is crossing your chest at a near vertical position. The elbow is down. *In this position the Kubotan always comes out of the bottom of the hand.*

Top of your hand :refers to the thumb and index finger when you're making a fist.

Bottom of your hand: refers to the little finger side of your hand when you're making a fist.

Quick change: refers to pushing the end of the Kubotan, in a lose gripped fist, so that it comes out of the top of the hand. Generally the push for a quick change can be against your own chest from a near chest position. But a quick change can occur by pushing against any part of your body or the assailant's body.

Step forward, back or to the side: refers to a deep stance that stabilizes your position, often in response to a push or a pull.

Palm direction helps you to understand the direction the Kubotan points and which way you are going to have to turn your hand in order to direct the Kubotan to your target. Palm facing left or right refers to your left or right. Palm down refers to the ground. Palm up refers to the sky. Sometimes I'll refer to 'palm facing you'.

- In order to prepare for the situational use of the Kubotan it's recommended that the twenty-three strike points be practiced with a partner. This exercise is called "walking the body".

- Hold the Kubotan so it protrudes from the bottom of your hand when you make a fist around it. (One end is flush with the thumb and index finger the other comes out past the little finger.)

STRIKE POINTS ON HEAD AND SHOULDERS

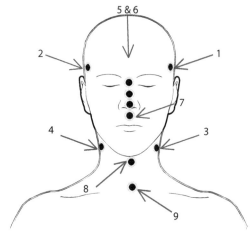

Begin with you and your partner facing each other.

1. **Left temple strike:** Take one step forward with your right foot, and extend your right arm straight so that the end of the Kubotan lines up on a horizontal plain with your partner's left temple. Your hand should end palm up.

2. **Right temple strike:** Retract your arm until it is near(referred to from now on as near chest) your chest, elbow down, arm nearly vertical. Throughout the next 9 moves the position of your feet never change. Now, extend your arm, palm down until the Kubotan is lined up with the right temple.

3. **Left side of the neck:** Retract your arm to near chest and extend it out, palm up, until the Kubotan lines up with the left side of the neck.

4. **Right side of the neck:** Retract your arm to near chest, and extend it out, palm down until the Kubotan lines up with the right side of the neck.

5. **Top of the bridge of the nose:** Retract the arm to near chest, and extend it in an arc, elbow pointing right, and direct the Kubotan to a point slightly below and between the eyes, palm down.

6. **Bridge of the nose:** Retract the arm to near chest, and extend it out in an arc, elbow pointing right, until the Kubotan is on a horizontal plain, and lined up with the bridge of the nose.

7. **Underneath the nose:** Retract the arm to near chest and extend it in an arc, elbow pointing right, until the Kubotan is on a horizontal plain, and lined up with the space directly below the nose.

8. **Underneath the chin:** Retract the arm to near chest, and extend it in a rising arc, rotating the hand so that the Kubotan extends up and strikes the soft tissue underneath and back slightly from the chin.

9. **Striking the middle throat:** Retract the arm to near chest and extend it out in and arc, elbow pointing right, hand palm down, until the Kubotan is on a horizontal plain and striking the middle of the throat.

KUBOTAN STRIKE POINTS

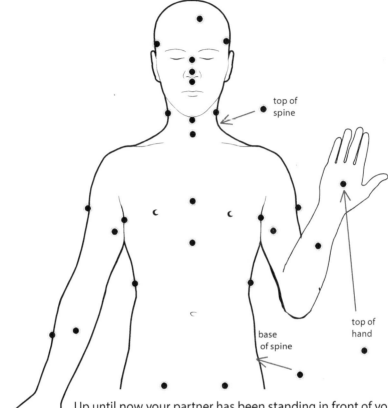

top of
spine

top of
hand

base
of spine

Up until now your partner has been standing in front of you with her hands at her sides. Now, when you have finished strike number nine, and retracted your arm to near chest she is to extend her arms to horizontal and directly out from her sides. To align yourself for the next five strikes step first with your left foot ten to twelve inches to your left and then with your right foot ten or twelve inches to your left. The goal is to be able to easily reach your partners out stretched arm from shoulder to hand, top and bottom of the arm.

10. **Top of the upper arm:** From near chest, extend your arm, palm facing left, so that the Kubotan strikes down on the top of the upper arm. The hand moves much like a hammer.

11. **Top of the forearm:** Retract your arm to near chest and then extend it, palm left, so that the Kubotan strikes down on the top of the forearm. The hand moves much like a hammer.

12. **Top of the hand:** Retract the arm to near chest, and then extend it so that the Kubotan strikes down on the top of the hand. The hand moves much like a hammer.

13. **Underneath the forearm:** Retract the arm to near chest, and then extend the arm in a rising arc, elbow pointing right. Rotate the hand counter clockwise until the Kubotan points up, and strike the underside of the forearm.

14. **Underneath the upper arm:** Retract the arm to near chest, and then extend it in a rising arc, turning the hand counter clockwise until the Kubotan points up and strikes the underside of the upper arm.

15. **Strike the arm pit:** Retract your arm to near chest, and then extend it, palm down, so that the Kubotan points right and moves on a horizontal plain until it strikes the arm pit.

    Now step back so that you are aligned with, or standing directly in front of, your partner again.

16. **Breast bone:** Retract your arm to near chest, and then extend it in an arc, palm down, until the Kubotan strikes the breast bone.

17. **Solar plexus:** Retract your arm to near chest, and then extend it in an arc, palm down, until the Kubotan strikes the solar plexus.

18. **Tip of the nose:** retract the arm to near chest, and then extend it in a slightly rising arch, palm down, until the Kubotan is on a horizontal plain and striking the tip of the nose.

19. **The Groin:** Retract the arm to near chest, then extend it in a falling arch. The elbow will point up slightly and the palm will face right and the Kubotan will strike at crotch level.

    For the next five moves you'll be adjusting your footing to strike various targets on the back and side of the torso. Your goal is to have a near straight arm when the Kubotan strikes its target.

20. **The floating ribs on the right side:** Retract your arm to near chest, then step adjusting your footing, strike in a falling arc, palm down, until the Kubotan strikes the floating ribs. The position of the strike would align with the seam in a shirt.

21. **The base of the spine:** Retract the arm to near chest, and then, stepping around, strike in a falling arc, palm down, until the Kubotan strikes the base of the spine. The target area would be on the spine at about belt level.

22. **The top of the spine:** Retract the arm to near chest, and then in a rising arc, palm down, strike the top of the spine with the Kubotan. The target is on the spine at the level of the collar.

23. **The floating ribs on the left side:** Retract the arm to near chest, and then adjusting your feet, extend your arm in a falling arc, palm down, until the Kubotan strikes the floating ribs. The position of the strike would align with the seam in a shirt.

Before you begin practicing strikes, read this:

- **Remember, thinking is slow**, and during a fast pace high adrenaline confrontation thinking will often become garbled.

- **For total clarity each attack is broken down** so at each step. you know what to do. I open each attack with the location of the Kubotan in relation to your body.

- **Next I describe the attack.** What the attacker is doing and where he is standing. Now, before you start review the terms for motion one more time. Becoming familiar with these terms means you won't need to think "how do I move my arm, how do I hold my hand? It will be automatic.

- **Read the directions through for each attack**, then, with a partner, walk through the moves slowly. If something doesn't make sense in practice, read the instruction again, then walk through it again, slowly. Sometimes it helps to have someone read the directions to make the walk through easier.

Important Tips:

1. **Don't improvise.** Most of these attack scenarios have been perfected over decades, and have proved very successful on the street.

2. **Don't cut corners, thinking you know what the next step will be.** Read each step, practice each step, develop muscle memory.

3. **Don't barrel through the various moves.** Go slow. Learn the strike zones. Memorize the terms.

4. **Choose your partner carefully.** He or she should grab push, or pull slowly to give you time to try out and learn the moves. As you become familiar with the various attacks your confidence will grow. You'll be more relaxed with the Kubotan and your partner will be able to push and grab more aggressively.

5. **Don't strike your partner with the Kubotan.** Pain and muscular spasm may occur and you'll quickly lose your partner. If you want to know what it feels like strike your own hand or inner arm. Beginning with a slow tapping, and then pull your hand back further and strike firmly.

Kubotan Strikes Against Attacks

1. **Grab to the left shoulder:**
   The Kubotan is held in a near chest position. The attacker grabs your left shoulder with his right hand. He may grip your shoulder or wad up your shirt in his fist in an attempt to control you. Respond immediately, extend your arm in a horizontal arc, palm up, striking the inside of his arm on or below the biceps.

   IF he does not let go at once, retract the arm to a near chest position, and step forward with your right foot, turn your hand to a palm down position and strike the side of his face. Turn and run.

2. **Push to the left shoulder:**
   The Kubotan is held in a near chest position. The attacker slams a right open hand into your left shoulder. Step forward with your right foot and deliver a right rising arc, palm up, striking the side of his head with the Kubotan.

   IF he does step away, retract the Kubotan to a near chest position and execute a falling arc, palm down, to his solar plexus. Turn and run.

3. **Grab to the center of the chest:** Your Kubotan was in a near chest position until the attacker made a grab to the center of the chest. He will likely wad up your clothing in his fist. Step back with your left foot, and deliver a returning arc, palm up, slamming the Kubotan into his neck or the top of his hand.

   IF he does not let go, reverse your hand position to palm down, and using his arm as a guide strike him in the side of the head. Turn and run.

4.   **Push to the center of the chest:**
     Keep your Kubotan to the right of a near chest position. You don't want him to dislodge the Kubotan from your grip, or grab the wrist of the hand that holds the Kubotan.

     Do not strike out. A flailing arm is something the attacker may latch onto. Do not resist the push. Instead, step back with your strong leg, turn and run.

5.   **Grab to the right shoulder:**
     The Kubotan is held in a near chest position. He may grab your shoulder or warp up your shirt in his fist. Execute a quick change. Use your body to push the Kubotan, allowing it to slide through your grip, until it sticks up above the thumb and index finger. Now in a rising arc, palm facing left, drive the Kubotan into the underside of his forearm.

     IF he doesn't let go retract the arm to a near chest position, palm down, punch the Kubotan into your chest for a quick change. Hold the Kubotan lightly so that it slides back out the bottom of your hand. Deliver a strike to the inside of his arm. Turn and run.

6.   **Push to the right shoulder:**
     Your Kubotan is held in a near chest position. Step forward with your left foot and extend your arm in an opening arc, palm down, striking the side of his head with the Kubotan. **IF** he doesn't step back, retract the Kubotan to a near chest position, and deliver in a falling arc, palm facing right, a strike to his stomach or groin. Turn and run

8. **Two handed grab to the chest:**
You have lowered the Kubotan from a near chest position. The attacker has grabbed your chest with both hands. Palm facing right, in a rising arc drive the Kubotan into the underside of either of his arms at the elbow. Now, retracting the Kubotan to a near stomach position, extend your arm out to your right, up over and down. Strike the top of either of his hands with the Kubotan.

IF he doesn't let go from the strike to the top of his hand drive the Kubotan up his arm to strike his face. Turn and run

8. **Right grab to your right wrist:**
The Kubotan is held so that an end sticks out of either side of your fist. The attacker has grabbed your right wrist with his right hand. Keeping your hand palm down turn your fist counter clockwise as far as possible. Now, tilt your hand until the Kubotan, where it sticks out from the bottom of the hand, is slightly higher then the wrist of the attacker.

Allow your wrist to straighten out simultaneously pressing down the tip of the Kubotan on the side of his Radius and pushing down until he releases his grip. Turn and run.

9. **Right grab to your left wrist:** Your Kubotan he held in a near chest position. The attacker has grabbed your left wrist with his right hand. Draw your right hand to the outside of your body and strike down, in a falling arc, palm facing left, striking the top of the attacker's hand with the Kubotan.

IF he does not let go turn your hand , palm facing down. Follow his arm up and strike to his face. Turn and run.

10. **Push to the face:** Retain your Kubotan in a near chest position. Do not resist the push, your attacker expects you to flail and panic. Instead, step back with your strong leg. Turn and run.

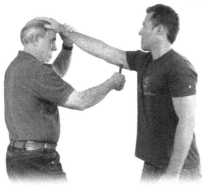

11. **Hair grab from the top front:**
    Your Kubotan is held in a near chest position. The attacker has grabbed a handful of hair on the top of your head. Execute a quick change with the Kubotan. **That is, push the Kubotan into your chest until it comes out the top of your hand.**

    Now, with a rising arc, palm facing roughly left, slam the Kubotan into the underside of his bicep. Without pause, with an extreme rising and falling arc, palm facing out, stab the Kubotan into the attackers hand that's holding your hair. Turn and run.

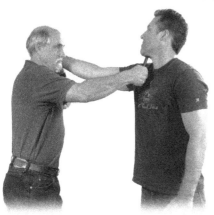

12. **Hair grab to the left side:**
    Your Kubotan is held in a near chest position. Your attacker has a hand full of your hair on the left side of the head. He may be standing in front of you or off to your left side.

    Do not attempt to strike his hand. Instead execute a quick change with the Kubotan so it now comes out of the top of your hand. Strike to the attackers forearm with the Kubotan and without pause, palm up strike to his face. Turn and run

13. Hair grab from the right side:

Your Kubotan is held in a near chest position. The attacker has a hand full of your hair from the right side of your head. He may be standing in front of you, or may be off to your right side.

Do not attempt to strike his hand. Instead with a right opening arc, palm down. Strike the inside of his right forearm with the Kubotan.

Now, without pause, retract the arm to near chest, and then straighten your arm and strike at his face. Turn and run.

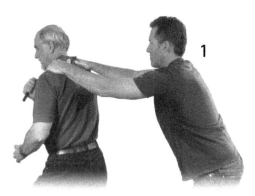

14. Two handed shoulder grab from behind:
Your Kubotan is held in a near chest position. The attacker has grabbed both shoulders or your neck from behind. You are surprised.

1. Step forward with your left foot (this will stretch out his arms)

2. Without moving your feet turn 180 degrees to your right, simultaneously driving your elbow straight up.

3. As you finish your turn drive your elbow down as though you were going to slam it into your own right hip. This move will push your elbow against his arms and possibly knock them lose. Whatever the case, his head will be in reach of your right hand. In an opening arc, palm down, strike the side of his head with the Kubotan. Turn and run.

15. **Head lock, attacker on the right side:** The Kubotan is held in a near chest position. The attacker surprises you with a headlock. Execute a quick change with the Kubotan so that it now comes out of the top of your hand.

    Drop your hand low and behind, and then with a rising arc, palm facing left bring the Kubotan into the attackers groin, without pause, draw the Kubotan back and slam it forward into the back of his nearest thigh. Stand up turn and run.

16. **Bear hug from the front your arms are pinned:** You saw the attacker coming but didn't anticipate the bear hug. You had brought the Kubotan into a near chest position. Your left hand is pinned at your side, your right hand pinned against your chest. Execute a quick change so that the end comes out of the top of your hand.

    Drive your right arm up, pushing the Kubotan into the soft underside of the attacker's chin.

17. **Bear hug from the front, your arms are free:** You saw the attacker coming but didn't anticipate the bear hug. Knocking your arms out of the way he grabs you in a bear hug, possibly lifting you off the ground.

    Execute a quick change with the Kubotan. In this case push against any available surface to push the Kubotan out the top of your hand. In a closing arc, palm down, strike the attackers head repeatedly. Turn and run.

18. Bear hug from behind, your arms are pinned:

Both your arms have been driven to your sides by the power of the attacker. Make him hold up your weight, and drive his encircling arms up by stepping deeply to your right with your right foot, simultaneously punching straight up with your arms.

The success of this move, so far, will be because **you responded immediately to his attack.** His encircling arms will have slid up until they are around your shoulders or loosely encircling your head. Bring your hands together directly in front of you, further raising his arms and switching the Kubotan from your right hand to your left.

Now in a falling arc, palm facing right, strike his groin or left thigh, and then drive your left elbow straight up striking his chin. Turn and run.

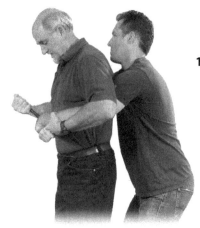

19. Bear hug from behind your arms are free:

The Kubotan is held in a near chest position. The attacker came up and encircled your body in a bear hug from behind in a total surprise to you. Your arms remain free. His grip will be a left hand over right or right over left, no matter. In a falling arc, palm facing you, slam the Kubotan into the top of his top hand. When his grip loosens, pry his hands apart, turn and run.

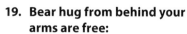

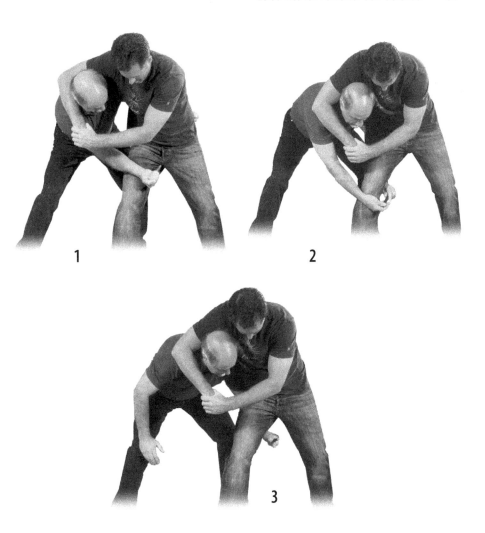

20. Headlock from the left side:

Your Kubotan is held in a near chest position. The attacker is standing on your left side.

1. Strike up between his legs with your left hand, immediately shooting it the rest of the way between his legs.

2. Bring your right and left hand together putting the Kubotan into your left hand.

3. Withdraw the left hand from between his legs, and then slam it into the back of his thigh. Stand up, turn and run.

A Final Word

The information in this book is intended to inform and alert you to the importance of being situationally aware and proactive in order to protect yourself and your loved ones from predators. Knowledge of an assailant's primary vulnerabilities and practice of a few simple defensive moves that take advantage of one or more of these vulnerabilities can give you an invaluable window for escape from harm. You may never need to use them, but with even a little practice you will be better prepared for an event that, unfortunately, happens to the majority people living in the United States at least once in their lifetime.

About the Author

My martial arts journey began over 45 years ago in Cupertino, California. The physical, mental, and spiritual teachings of the arts have been a common thread throughout my life. To date I hold a 3rd degree Black Belt in Chinese Kenpo Karate and the equivalent in two other Chinese styles. I've studied extensively in traditional Japanese sword and a variety of styles of stick, including Arnis, Jo and Kubotan.

Somewhere in the 1980's, after instructing law enforcement in San Jose, California, Phoenix, Arizona, and owning and operating martial art schools in several states, I became aware of the need for a practical self-defense system. This lead me to develop Tactical Kenpo, a series of 80 abbreviated Kenpo moves. Tactical Kenpo is an easily learned system of explosive self-defense techniques that will stop aggression and allow escape. The strategies in book, *Survival Self-Defense* and *Tactical Kubotan*, are in the spirit of Tactical Kenpo—simple and practical self-defense that anyone can learn.

One of my greatest joys comes from instructing students in self-defense using this book as a basic guide. My greatest pride is the contribution of Tactical Kenpo to the martial arts community and that I can give back something to a tradition that has given me so much.

NOTES

NOTES

CPSIA information can be obtained
at www.ICGtesting.com
Printed in the USA
LVHW052349030321
680485LV00013B/1971